Mix-up

It is morning. Dad is sorting
out the tops, socks and shorts.

2

Dad picks up a top with a fort on it. It is a bit torn.

Dan's or Sam's? I think it's Sam's.

Then he picks up a top with a horn on it. It looks worn out.

Nat's or Dan's? It might be Nat's.

Then he looks at the socks.
He picks up a pink sock and
a sock with corn cobs on it.

Dad picks up red shorts.
He thinks they are Sam's,
or they might be Dan's.

Dad has sorted it all.

But then Sid thinks he sees a good bed!

Get off, Sid!

Sid hops off and it is
all a bit of a mess.

Sam gets his things.

Nat picks up her things.

Dan picks his up too.

Dan and Sam are back to see Dad.

Nat is back too.

Oh! This is not right!

Words to blend

shorts	think	this
epic	thanks	pink
looks	good	might
tight	right	sees
too	long	mess
bed	things	odd
picks	then	mix-up

Before reading

Synopsis: Dad is sorting the clean laundry. He puts the clothes in separate piles for the three children. Does he get it right? Is Sid helping?

Review grapheme/phoneme: ar

New grapheme/phoneme: or

Story discussion: Look at the cover, and read the title together. Ask: *What do you think Dad is doing? Have you ever helped with sorting the laundry?*

Link to prior learning: Display the grapheme *or*. Say: *These two letters are a digraph – that means they make one sound.* Write or display these words: *form, port, corn, fork.* How quickly can children identify the *or* grapheme and read the words?

Vocabulary check: epic – a colloquial term meaning big or amazing

Decoding practice: Display the word *sorting*. Show children how to split it into syllables *(s-or-t/i-ng)* and then sound out and blend each syllable in turn in order to read the word.

Tricky word practice: Display the word *my* and ask children to circle the tricky part of the word (*y*, which makes an /igh/ sound). Practise writing and reading this word.

After reading

Apply learning: Ask: *How did Dad's feelings change in the story? How do you think he was feeling at the end?*

Comprehension

- How did the clothes get mixed up again?

- How do you think Dad feels at the end of the story?

- Can you think of a way to stop the clothes getting mixed up next time?

Fluency

- Pick a page that most of the group read quite easily. Ask them to reread it with pace and expression. Model how to do this if necessary.

- Ask children to turn to pages 14–15 and read the speech bubbles with lots of expression.

- Practise reading the words on page 17.

Tricky words review

out	and	I
he	be	all
are	go	they
me	her	my
was	oh	for